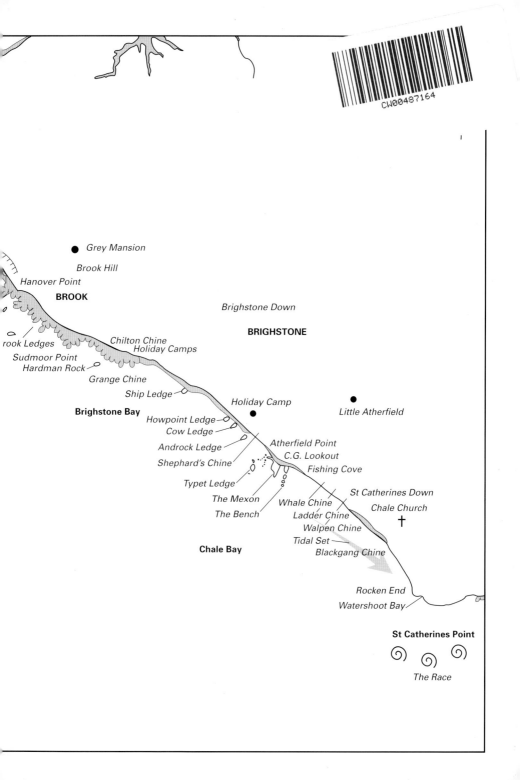

Grey Mansion

Brook Hill

Hanover Point

BROOK

Brighstone Down

BRIGHSTONE

Chilton Chine
Holiday Camps

rook Ledges

Sudmoor Point
Hardman Rock

Grange Chine

Ship Ledge

Holiday Camp

Brighstone Bay

Little Atherfield

Howpoint Ledge

Cow Ledge

Androck Ledge

Atherfield Point

C.G. Lookout

Shephard's Chine

Fishing Cove

Typet Ledge

St Catherines Down

The Mexon

Whale Chine

Chale Church

The Bench

Ladder Chine

Walpen Chine

Tidal Set

Chale Bay

Blackgang Chine

Rocken End

Watershoot Bay

St Catherines Point

The Race

WIGHT

HAZARDS

Peter Bruce

First edition published June 1987
Second edition published December 1989
Reprinted June 1995
Reprinted July 1998
Third edition published July 2001
Fourth Edition published May 2008

Other pilotage books by the same author:

Solent Tides
Solent Hazards
Inshore Along the Dorset Coast
Tidal Streams between Portland Bill and St Alban's Head

BOLDRE MARINE
Kestrel Cottage • Shirley Holms • Lymington • Hampshire • SO41 8NH • UK
Telephone & Fax 01590683106

CONTENTS

Acknowledgement
Few would have the temerity to publish a book such as this without the help of local expertise. I have obtained much valuable information by consulting those who live on the Island coast and I am grateful to these good people for answering my questions with typical Island patience and courtesy. I'm also grateful to those learned people who read the proofs, and the skilful pilots who fly me around to take the photographs.

Caution
While every care has been taken in compiling this book, it is regretted that no responsibility can be taken by the author or publisher for inaccuracies or omissions, or for any accidents or mishaps resulting from its use.

Design by David Rose
Printed in China through Printworks Int. Ltd.

Front cover
A hazard off St Catherine's lighthouse.

Back Cover
Bembridge Harbour channel, 13 April 07.
Nae man can tether time or tide.
Photo ©Mike Samuelson

1 THE SOUTH COAST OF THE ISLE OF WIGHT – INTRODUCTION

The southern shores of the Isle of Wight have their own special charms and hazards. The coasts are exposed to the full force of channel gales, which bring bigger seas than in the Solent, overfalls, dangerous lee shores and that more subtle foe, the swell. As might be expected there can be a marked difference between the shelter offered by the coastline facing the prevailing wind and that on the eastern side.

Though there are no large scale charts for much of the coast, inlets such as Scratchell's, Luccombe and Priory Bays are well worth a visit when the weather is right (and the tide at Priory Bay). The water is clearer than in the Solent, bird life is more prolific, fishing is richer and there is seldom a crowd. In addition, the Island coast makes a corner in a shipping route and, having been once a centre of piracy and smuggling, it has much of historical interest.

A few old wrecks present a risk to vessels going near the shore, and there are several rocks and ledges that have wrought the destruction of a large number of vessels over the years, particularly in winter and before the invention of radar. At the turn of the century the exposed coast lying between the Needles and St Catherine's Point, known locally as the Back of the Wight, warranted no less than three rowing lifeboats in the space of six miles: one stationed at Brook, another at Brighstone and the third at Atherfield.

To cover the hazards of the outer Island coast, an imaginary voyage will be taken anticlockwise around the south of the Island from the Needles Channel, round St Catherine's Point to No Man's Land Fort. Place names are taken from local sources, Admiralty charts numbers 2035, 2037, and 2045, and the Ordnance Survey map (Outdoor Leisure 29) of 2 inches to 1 mile scale, which is accurate and detailed between mean high and mean low water, and therefore is a valuable aid when landing. There are a few instances where charts are at variance with this book though, one notices, fewer with the passage of time as chart corrections are made. These variations are reflected in the text and, usually, photographic evidence puts the matter beyond dispute.

For convenience, all compass bearings are given in degrees magnetic (M), and a variation of 3° west is assumed. Tidal heights given in the text are taken from chart datum.

1

An overhead view of the Needles. Goose Rock can be seen at 10 o'clock from the lighthouse and the four dangerous hunks of wreck can be seen further out, in line with the lighthouse and the Needles rocks.

It is well known that numerous craft have been badly damaged by hitting the wreck of the *Varvassi* off the Needles (Plate 1). Less well known is that the critical remnants of the wreck are on a chalk ledge, which extends westwards on the same line as the present Needles Rocks towards the Bridge buoy. Steep breaking waves form over this ledge but there is a short stretch of water to the west of the wreck that can be a good deal less uncomfortable. As it is difficult to judge distance off when rounding the Needles lighthouse, it is wise to give the wreck and the ledge a wide berth. A rule of thumb, used by open fishing boats to give a depth of at least 3m, is to make

sure the lighthouse's main light will be buried in the coastguard station at West High Down before the Needles come into line. Vessels with greater height of eye will need to keep further out. The inner passage is only for the bold and knowledgeable; nevertheless, if the swirl of water over Goose Rock and the inner of the *Varvassi's* boilers can be identified, when heading from the Solent to the open sea, the deepest water will be found by leaving Goose Rock about ten metres to port and then heading south. There will then be some 3m at chart datum on the best

2

A view of the inshore passage between the eastern boiler of the wreck and Goose Rock where many craft have come to grief. The *Varvassi* went aground on 5 January 1947.

line and some 2.4m on the worst (Plate 2). It is not advisable to take this passage for the first time whilst racing. Two yachts in the 2007 Round the Island Race hit some rusty metal object in the gap, possibly structure of the *Varvassi* wreck.

The third option, of course, when negotiating this point, is to 'thread the Needles'. Though this route is quite commonly undertaken by fishing craft, it is advisable only in shallow drafted craft under power in calm conditions with no swell. In 1627 two Dutch East Indiamen tried to do so when unable to weather the Needles,

and both had their bottoms torn out in the process. The remains of one of them, the *Campen,* still lie on the south side of the middle Needle while the other called *Vliegende Draecke* had to be beached.

The best time to thread the Needles is at slack water, bearing in mind that the tide is not slack for long and can run at a tremendous rate. It is usually just possible at low water in a dinghy, and whilst there is more scope at high water, one must remember that the tidal range at the Needles is only about two metres at springs and one metre at neaps, as opposed to four metres at springs and two metres at neaps at Portsmouth (Plate 3).

One can negotiate both gaps

3

The Needles viewed from the north. The places to thread the Needles are where there are gaps in the white foam.

4

The inner gap of the Needles is virtually blocked.

between the Needles, but only canoeists can just manage the gap between the Needles and the Island shore (Plate 4). Old prints show this inner gap as an archway, and it seems that when the arch collapsed it mostly blocked the passage. It is advisable, of course, to head into any current that is running, at least until familiar with the best line. When the tide is flooding, the water level is visibly higher in Scratchell's Bay, so going with the current is like shooting rapids into nasty overfalls and white water.

The westernmost passage, i.e. the gap between the two outer Needles, has the deepest water in the centre and has one prominent rock, northwest of the middle point, to be avoided. When this rock is just showing above the surface, at least one metre will be found elsewhere. There is another

The outer gap of the Needles at low water spring tide.

The middle gap of the Needles at low water spring tide.

rock, just south of the western end of the middle Needle, which is just about awash at low water springs (Plate 5).

The passage between the middle and inner Needle is wider and more generally used. All the most prominent submerged rocks obstructing the channel are on the north side, and the best line lies about one third of the width of the gap from the middle Needle, leaving one rock to the west and the other two to the east. The westernmost rock

The Needles

7

Cleopatra's Needle viewed from Scratchell's Bay beach taken from a map published on 20 August 1759.

is the highest, and if its position is in doubt it is safer to err towards the middle of the gap (Plate 6). It was at the western side of this gap that the 40m high pencil of rock called Cleopatra's Needle, or Lot's Wife, stood until it collapsed spectacularly in 1764 (Plate 7). Early 17th century charts show a cluster of similar pencil-shaped chalk stacks on the northwest side of what we call the Needles, and it seems that Cleopatra's Needle was the last of them to go. One of these old charts shows a sketch of 14 such chalk stacks as well as an additional 'tooth', shaped much like the present Needles, at the position where the dangerous remains of the *Varvassi* now lie. The white pencils of rock in addition to the present Needles must have been a remarkable sight, and must presumably account for the name.

If landing at the lighthouse (and permission should first be obtained from Trinity House), one should approach from the northwest, leaving Goose Rock close to starboard before turning to port to go alongside the steps. A deep-water channel exists between Goose Rock and the spit on which the lighthouse stands, and this makes a clean approach, but a tricky one when the tide is running.

Once into Scratchell's Bay (Plate 8) – the name originating from Old Scratch, one of the Devil's many pseudonyms – there are two large offlying perils to watch for: St Anthony Rock and Irex Rock. Of these two, St Anthony Rock, named after the

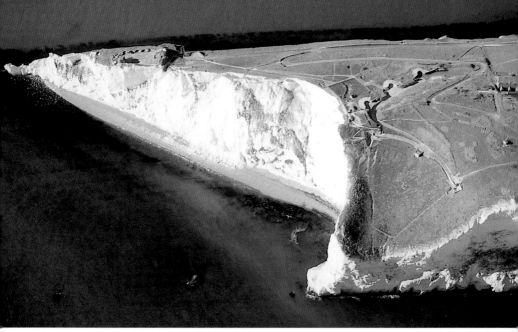

8 (above)

Scratchell's Bay looking northeast. Sun Corner Rock, St Anthony Rock and Irex Rock can be seen.

9 (below)

A closer view of Scratchell's Bay looking east with, in the foreground, a rare view of Irex Rock uncovered.

treasure ship wrecked there in 1691, is the more obvious, being visible and usually surrounded by breaking water.

But Irex Rock, named after a new full-rigged ship that went aground upon it on the stormy night of 26 January

10

Irex Rock is on a line with the highest point of
St Anthony Rock and the cave behind in Sun Corner,
known as the Needles Cave. Note that Old Pepper
Rock is just beginning to show from behind the base
of the cliff.

11

A view of the dry moat wall from Irex Rock.

1890, is of more interest to navigators,
being further offshore and only just
awash at chart datum (Plate 9). It will
be found by steering down the transit
of the highest point of St Anthony
Rock and the cave behind, on a course
of 085°M (Plate 10), until the Old
Needles Battery dry moat wall is in
line on 027°M (Plate 11); but great
care should be taken as solid rock rises
steeply from 8m of water (Plate 12).
Photographic evidence and bearings
put Irex a little northeast of the inner
of the two rocks shown on the chart to
the west of St Anthony, and there is
only the one Irex Rock to be found,
rather than the two shown on the
chart. Divers report that much debris
from the Irex, especially iron pipes from
her cargo, still lie around the rock.

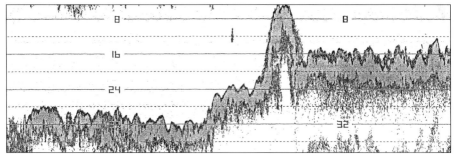

12 (above)

A bottom contour obtained an hour before high water, showing Irex Rock when approached from seaward towards the dry wall in line. Soundings are in feet.

13

Scratchell's Bay on a calm day.

14

A rare view of Sun Corner Rock exposed.

In calm weather the pebble beach at Scratchell's Bay can make a delightfully secluded and sunny picnic spot, overlooked only by sea birds (Plate 13). It is best to land towards Sun Corner around high water but beware if any swell is running. Apart from rocks along the shore opposite St Anthony Rock, there is a rock off Sun Corner, awash at low water springs, with deep enough water close inside it for very small craft (Plate 14). It is well

15
When Old Pepper Rock is fully in view from behind the Main Bench cliffs, a vessel will be clear of all the rocks in Scratchell's Bay.

to the north of the rock shown on the chart off Sun Corner.

After a period of heavy winter rainfall major landslides take place from the cliffs, usually in the centre of the bay. Though the cliff falls block the beach, the soft chalk soon washes away.

When passing Scratchell's Bay one can avoid Irex and St Anthony Rock by keeping Old Pepper Rock in full view when sighting down the line of the cliffs to the east of Sun Corner, known as the Main Bench (Plate 15). From Sun Corner on towards Old Pepper Rock the white flinty chalk cliffs initially plunge straight into deep water (Plate 16). However, there is a rock off

17 (below)

16 (above)

It is safe to approach the Main Bench cliffs closely just east of Scratchell's Bay.

Looking north at Old Pepper Rock. Bench Rock can be seen on the left of Old Pepper Rock and there are numerous other rocks on all sides which dry, or nearly dry, at low water spring tides.

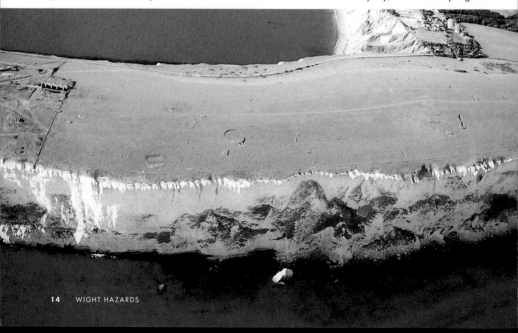

18

A close up view of Old Pepper Rock.

the cliff some 300m west of Old Pepper Rock which does not quite dry. Furthermore the seaweed-covered Bench Rock about 200m west of Old Pepper dries over a metre, and there are many other rocks within 200m of both sides of Old Pepper Rock itself (Plate 17). One can be well clear of all of this by keeping the Needles lighthouse in view to the left of Sun Corner, though with a strong ebb tide and a westerly wind a tidal race will be felt off the point.

Old Pepper Rock (a hundred years ago it was just called Pepper Rock) is the principal feature of this piece of coast (Plate 18). From offshore of Old Pepper a ledge runs east in a smooth curve all the way to Compton Bay. Passage inside this ledge is ever interesting and adventurous, as the bottom is distinctly uneven. Moreover, the outlying rocks and ledges are not easily identified from seaward except by the presence of lobster pots.

19

Wedge Rock is found just to the east of Old Pepper Rock.

Consequently yachts are seldom seen in here and even the larger fishing boats avoid this coast. It is helpful to know that lobster pots are often laid either side of the principal rocks and in strings along the ledge.

East of Old Pepper Rock more rocks appear at low water springs up to

20

Kitchen, Parlour and Cellar Caves viewed from the air.

50m offshore beyond Wedge Rock (Plate 19). The caves marked on the chart as Kitchen, Parlour and Cellar were so named because a colourful gentleman called Lord Holmes surprisingly used them for the entertainment of his guests (Plate 20). Lord Holmes was a buccaneering naval commander, whose plundered gold from West Africa probably gave rise to the guinea coin. He became captain and the first governor of the Isle of Wight in 1668 and his tomb and marble statue can be found in Yarmouth's pretty little church. The story goes that the almost-completed statue had been carved for the figure of Louis XIV and was being shipped to the king in France, complete with the sculptor, so the king's facial features would be correct. Robert Holmes, somewhat in the tradition of

previous captains of the Isle of Wight, took over the ship and contents, possibly after it had been wrecked when by tradition he had 'rights of wreck', and the sculptor was obliged to finish the statue in Holmes's likeness (Plate 21).

21

King Louis XIV's marble statue, appropriated by Lord Holmes and finished with his own features.

22

A view from Old Pepper Rock towards the Yar River.
Kitchen, Parlour and Cellar Caves can be seen in
the centre of the page and Frenchman's Hole at
about the same distance to the east.

23

The cliffs adjacent to Tennyson's monument. Frenchman's hole is to be seen on the left as well as a submerged ledge, which follows the curvature of the cliffs at some distance to seaward.

Intrepid explorers will find The Cellar the easiest of the caves to enter, being free of rocks when approached from the west. From these caves and on past Frenchman's Hole (Plate 22) the shore is relatively clean.

There are several high points on the ledge that appear at low water. One such is Tank Rock, so called because there is a rusty red, bullet-riddled water tank on the cliff behind. It lies between New Ditch and Tennyson's Monument. The latter bears 041°M from Tank Rock when viewed from a distance, but from anywhere close to, the cliff face hides the monument. From Tank Rock, Old Pepper bears 265° M, the fence on the top of the cliff bears 288°M, and the tank itself bears 337° M (Plate 23)

24
The cliffs from Tennyson's Monument to Freshwater Bay.

25
Watcombe Bay and part of Freshwater Bay.

Past Tennyson's Monument comes Adder Rock, now shown again on the chart. This is another high point on the ledge exposed at low water, with no obvious transits to locate it. Bearings to the extreme left-hand edge of Tennyson Cliff on 263° M and Chilton Chine (chine is the local word for a ravine or cleft in the cliff) on 115°M give its approximate position; moreover Black Rock, a conspicuous dark stone perched on a plinth at the bottom of the cliff, is about 300m to the east of the Adder on a bearing of 070°M. Another drying high point on the ledge bears 196°M from Black Rock (Plate 24).

Before arriving at Freshwater Bay, there is a smaller rocky inlet called Watcombe Bay, with two tall rocks towards the west end (Plate 25). Though only worth a visit at high water, it has the attraction of being inaccessible from landward. The well-covered wreck 400m to the southwest of Watcombe Bay is that of the armed merchant vessel *War Knight*, (Plate 26) which was deliberately sunk by gunfire in 1918, after being in collision with an American tanker carrying naphtha and hitting a mine. Amongst other cargo, she was carrying bacon and lard, and this became a welcome addition to the war-restricted local food supply when it was washed up on the beach. Though well broken up the wreck is still a popular diving site.

26

The *War Knight* ablaze off Watcombe Bay in March 1918.

27
Freshwater Bay in evening light.

Freshwater Bay, sometimes locally called Freshwater Gate, is the marine centre, such as it is, of the south-west Island coast and the base for an inshore 8.8m RIB lifeboat. It might be useful to know that the lifeboat carries a copy of *Wight Hazards* on board. With little protection from the south it is by no means a safe anchorage, nor always a safe beach for swimming (Plate 27). In summertime three or four fishing craft lie at moorings opposite the Albion Hotel on the most sheltered west side of the

harbour, but before the onset of bad weather they have either to be hauled up the beach or be taken round to Yarmouth. In 1988 several boats capsized at their moorings in unforeseen gales, and one broke up on the beach.

The bay is shallow at low water and rocky on both sides of the entrance, which is a gap in the chalk ledge that was enlarged with explosives to allow the escape of the full rigged ship *Carl,* driven ashore in a gale in 1916. The best line to enter the bay is on a bearing of 009° M towards a yellowish brick wall in line. Though visiting craft are made welcome, the shingle bottom is not good holding ground and one should not try to go in if there is an onshore wind of more than force 4, or any swell. If forced to land in unfavourable conditions the best place is on the beach, as far to the west of the moorings as possible.

Stag and Mermaid Rocks lie on a shelf of rocks to the east of the inlet (Plate 28). Arch Rock, the erstwhile splendid feature of Freshwater Bay, collapsed in the severe gale of 25 October 1992. There is a ledge of isolated rocks further on to the east and these are awash at chart datum, but none now dry quite as much as 0.9m, which the chart suggests. A clearing bearing is 309° M on the left-hand edge of Stag Rock. The beach behind the offshore rocks is called Butter Bay. It is not easily accessible from the cliff top and makes an interesting landing place in placid weather. As at Watcombe Bay it is much easier to land at high water when the rocks are covered.

28 (below)

Stag and Mermaid Rocks with the two stumps of the erstwhile Arch Rock between them. Butter Bay is behind Mermaid rock.

29

The northeast corner of Compton Bay, showing Old House Reef.

Compton Bay is a shallow, rather desolate sandy bight (Plate 29). Old House Reef lies along the north shore under what used to be called Afton Cliff, ending at Compton Corner, the point where white and brown cliffs merge. There are dangerous ledges at the south end of the bay that extend well out to sea from Brook Point, or Hanover Point as it is also called. At a place called Shippard's Chine at the extreme north of Brook Ledges, on a bearing of 317°M from the cairn on the ledge off Brook Point, is the wreck of a 185 ton Admiralty steam tug number C150, built in 1896, called *Carbon*. She lost her tow off St Aldhelm's (Alban's) head and drifted ashore opposite High Grange when bound for the breakers' yard in November 1947 (Plate 30).

The cairn, locally called the Thimble (Plates 31 and 32), was built in 1911 out of concrete filled sandbags. It was designed to mark the eastern limit of arc of fire for the quick firing 6 and 12 pounder battery at Fort Redoubt, located on the western side of Freshwater Bay. Brook Point (Plate 33), as with all this soft and exposed coastline, erodes apace, indeed an *average* of a yard a year is the traditional figure, usually in chunks 10-15 yards at a time. When Brooke Point was rather closer to

30 (above)

Shippard's Chine with the wreck of the Carbon to be seen in the centre, at right angles to the ledges.

31 (below)

The Thimble looking northwest.

32 (above)
The Thimble from the air, looking south east.

33 (below)
Brook (or Hanover) Point, looking northeast. The access road to the beach can be seen within the bay, on the right.

the Thimble than now, the Navy used the cliff as a target for gunnery practice. A 32 pound cannon was sited on the east side of Brook Bay, somewhere on the cliff opposite the old lifeboat house, and 32 pound cannon balls may still be found in the pools between the Thimble and the shore. Rock strata run east/west off the point, so the ledges dry at low water springs in parallel lines.

There is no easy guide for keeping clear of Brook Ledges. At night it is safest to keep to the west of a line between the Needles and St Catherine's lighthouses. If one has the visibility and can judge it, keeping west of a line between Tennyson's Monument and St Catherine's Point is safe. A less conservative clearing line is given by keeping the Needles lighthouse in full view from behind Sun Corner. Prudence is necessary when using this line, as it will take a vessel over the outer ledges. Moreover, just south of Chilton Chine less than two metres will be found, and rather less than this off Ship Ledge. It is worth noting that the water turns brown over the reefs in anything but the calmest conditions, and whilst inshore fishermen find this change of colour a useful indication of shoal waters, deep-keeled yachts should treat it as an absolute final warning.

Though this coast is notoriously unfriendly in a southwesterly blow, it is enjoyable to thread through the wilderness of rocks by dinghy in calm weather at low water. Past the rocks off Brook Point, some of which are fossilised pine trees, and heading southeast for St Catherine's Point, there is the partly rock-free inlet of Brook Bay from which a small number of fishing boats operate. A conspicuous large building described as 'Grey Mansion' on old charts, less poetically 'House' on new charts, and Brook Hill House on the OS map, serves as a useful reference when entering Brook Bay. Pick up the bearing of 056°M on this building when offshore of Brook Ledges, then proceed cautiously into the bay until the shore features are visible, when one should 'come up the road' as the locals say, on a bearing of 063° M, meaning come in on the line of the emergency approach road to the

34

Looking 'up the road' at Brook Bay.

launching area (Plate 34). Once into the bay, one will be rewarded by finding a sandy beach at low water or a pleasant high water picnic anchorage at a place that appears on the chart to be nothing but a tangle of ledges.

Entering Brook Bay at low water, one will see rocks dried out to starboard, further to seaward of the main reef called Stag Rocks, with the group

35 (above)

Brook Ledges, looking southeast. Sovereign Rocks on the right.

36 (below)

Brook Ledges, looking northeast.

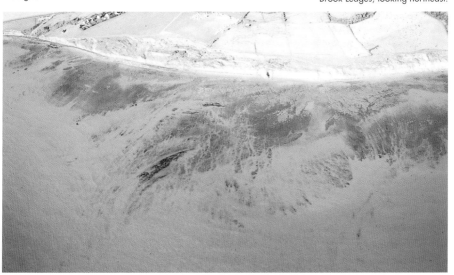

inshore known as the Little Stag Rocks. For two miles south of Brook Bay the inshore ledges are prominent, some curved but mostly running at right angles to the shore (Plates 35 and 36). The beach looks less rocky as one goes further east to Atherfield, but ledges still exist though more deeply sub- merged. There are salient ledges off Sudmoor Point, and off Chilton Chine (Plate 37) where the waves tumble especially steeply. Incidentally, the sandstones of the 'undercliff' along this shore are of geological interest, especially as erosion continues to expose fossilised dinosaurs, as well as the odd bronze

37 (above)

Ledges off Chilton Chine. Hardman Rock is on the left in the foreground.

38 (above)

A closer view of Hardman Rock.

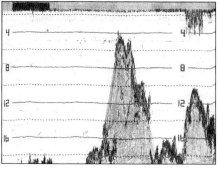

39 (above)

An echo sounder bottom trace showing how steep the seaward face of Hardman Rock is. Soundings are in feet.

age pot holding cremated remains. If walking along the beach from Brook Point past Crab Pool and Taylor's Rocks to Chilton Chine, or vice versa, one should be careful not to become cut off by the rising tide.

Hardman Rock (Plate 38) locally pronounced Harman, is now shown on most recent charts. (It seems increasingly likely that somebody must have been reading this book.) The rock is well offshore and drops 3.5m on its vertical leading edge so it is the most dangerous hazard on this stretch of coastline (Plate 39). It is found half a mile west of the large house at Chilton Chine. There is a useful transit on 082° M, formed by the TV tower at Chillerton in line with the right hand window of the lower right building adjoining the large house to the south

of Chilton Chine (Plate 40). Thus, keeping the TV tower to the right of the wall clears Hardman Rock. From

40 (above)
A transit of the Chillerton TV tower with the right hand window of the building on a bearing of 082° M marks Hardman Rock.

41 (below)
Ledges east of Chilton Chine looking northeast.

42 (above)

Ship Ledge looking northeast.

43 (below)

Ship Ledge with ship.

the rock Brook Hill House bears 354° M, and the Thimble 309° M, the latter in line with a whiter patch at the western end of Afton Cliffs, just before the trees appear on the skyline.

East of Chilton Chine the large offshore ledges peter out (Plate 41) but another hazard, Ship Ledge, will be found a mile southeast of Chilton Chine (Plates 42 and 43). From offshore of this ledge the TV tower at Chillerton bears about 068° M, otherwise it has no particular shore feature to mark it. On the chart it is now named and shown as a spit with 0.9m depth. The ledge can be avoided by keeping to seaward of a line through Brook and Sudmoor Points on 308° M; or by keeping a whole west Needle rock in view as well as the lighthouse or, less conservatively, by keeping the low lying Albion Hotel in view at Freshwater.

44 (above)
Howpoint, Cow and Androck Ledges off Cowleaze and Shepherd's Chines on the left. Atherfield Ledge on the right.

45
Atherfield Ledge, looking northeast.

This applies to the smaller ledges, Howpoint Ledge, and Cow Ledge further towards Atherfield (Plate 44). Behind these ledges lie uniform cliffs famous for fossils and slippery clay.

Atherfield Ledge (Plate 45) consists of two groups of rocks which dry out up to 400m offshore. To the west is The Mexon, a slab of rock 200m by 80m, and to the east The Bench, a narrower ledge that, well submerged, extends some miles out into the bay. The unlit Atherfield buoy was removed on 7 August 1988 for reasons of economy but the position of the ledge can usually still be identified by the tide race running over The Bench. This can be quite fierce at spring tides.

The Atherfield Ledges were amongst the most notorious of the Island hazards in the days of sailing ships, and there is a confusion of plates and beams from fine craft such as the *Auguste*, the *Alcester* and the *Sirenia* scattered between the rocks of the ledge. Many vessels have been lost along this coast in fog. In addition, if a square-rigged vessel failed to make enough offing at St Catherine's Point in a strong onshore wind, she would have insufficient windward ability to sail out of Chale Bay, thus ending up on Atherfield Ledge.

Beyond Atherfield there are four chines – namely, from north to south: Whale, Ladder, Walpen and New Chine (Plate 46). To avoid going aground on Atherfield Ledge when working along the shore, local fishermen keep outside a line between Walpen Chine and Chale Church, with its white flagstaff. Yachtsmen with deep keels will want to give the ledge a wider berth, especially if a sea is running. More generous clearance of Atherfield Ledge is given by keeping

46

From left to right: Whale, Ladder, Walpen and New Chines. A fair weather transit for small vessels to avoid Atherfield Ledge is to keep to the southwest of a line between the Chale village church and Walpen Chine.

outside the line of Brook Point and the highest part of the white chalk of Afton Cliff (to the east of Freshwater Gate) on 319° M.

Just to the east of Atherfield there is a cove where the lifeboat used to be launched. This was also the home of a dozen or more fishing boats although not so many are to be seen there now (Plate 47). As might be expected on a shore where erosion is rampant, old maps show Atherfield as more prominent, thereby giving more protection to the cove. The steep beach is still a surprisingly sheltered landing place, especially at low water when the ledge's screening effect is more pronounced. Care should be taken to avoid the numerous fish float lines just offshore.

On 6 February 1910 a new Belgian steam trawler called the *Nemrod* came ashore in fog south of Atherfield. Her seaweed-covered boiler lies about 100m off Walpen Chine and is awash at low water spring tide.

47

The fishing fleet just to the southeast of Atherfield Ledge.

The east end of the long beach of Chale Bay (Plate 48) with its interesting rock formations and crumbling cliff (Plates 49 and 50) is popular with people for whom beach clothing is optional. They are known locally as

48 (above)

New Chine and the cliffs at Chale Bay.

49 (below)

Blackgang Chine, where the village is seriously affected by cliff erosion.

50 (above)

The view of Blackgang Bluff from below.

Blackgang Bares and live in caravans half way up the cliff. The beach finishes at Rocken End (Plates 51–54) where the distinctive Shag Rock used to be, with the shape and size of an African mud hut; but it was turned over in the storm of 25 January 1980 and now looks less distinguished, though large. It is the start of a wild and rockbound coast where there are no easy landing places at low water until one comes to

Sandown Bay. Local divers report that the uncharted wreck of the *Wheatfield*, a steamer that went ashore in 1882, lies 200m due west of Shag Rock, opposite the naturists' caravans. Her two large and solid boilers stand 4m above the seabed in a charted depth of about 8m of water; though probably not presenting a hazard to vessels likely to be that close in, they might well give a twinge to someone looking at an echo sounder.

51

Rocken End, looking northeast. The largest rock is Shag rock.

52 (above)

Rocken End, looking east.

53 (below)

Rocken End, looking east from sea level.

54 (above)

Rocken end, looking north from sea level.

55 (below)

Watershoot Bay from overhead. The left hand outer dry rock is Shark Rock and the second outer dry rock, in the middle of the picture, is the rock illustrated in Plate 57.

Immediately to the southeast of Rocken End is an inlet called Watershoot Bay (Plate 55), a pretty rock cove possibly named after a sloop lost there in 1755. It would seem rare

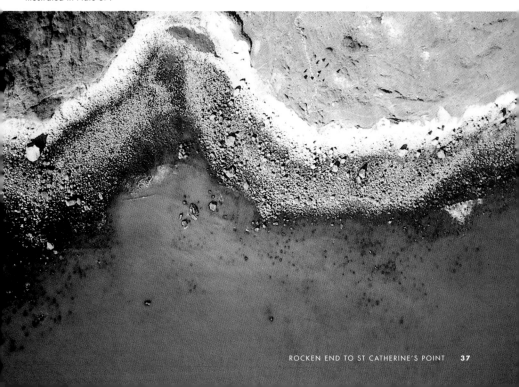

56 (above)

Shark Rock. Notice that the left hand edge of Shag Rock is in line with Freshwater Bay.

to have the right weather to land, yet in the past fishermen and smugglers used to operate from here. Entry is very difficult, with the best approach from the northwest at high water, leaving Shark Rock, which is surrounded by deep water, to starboard (Plate 56). The best bit of beach for landing is in the southeast corner. From Shark Rock, which looks rather like a shark's dorsal fin on the rare occasions that it is uncovered, St Catherine's light bears 098° M and Shag Rock 308° M. Shark Rock has 2.4m depth around it when just exposed, so no warning will be given on the echo sounder. To be clear of it, keep Shag Rock to the right of the chalk cliffs on the east side of Freshwater Bay.

Further south, off-lying rocks can be seen when St Catherine's Point bears

57

The submerged unnamed outlying rock south of Shark Rock. Notice that Shag Rock is in line with the white cliffs of Afton Down to the east of Freshwater Bay.

093° M (Plate 57) and 049° M – West St Cat's Rock – but nothing shows above water at the point indicated on the chart as Jeremy Rock. In 1752 there is a record of a sloop being cast upon 'Jersey' Rock in the immediate area; a map published in 1826 shows 'Jerome' Rock as an island of some 100m diameter in the present charted position of Jeremy Rock, and there is an account of the London steamer *Cayo Soto* running aground just outside the Jeremy Rock on 24 October 1908. Admiralty charts, such as that of 1852, show Jeremy Rock as a drying rock one cable offshore with an outline but no drying height, whereas modern charts give it the symbol of a drying rock, but again no drying height.

Though some later charts show Jeremy Rock in a different position, just to seaward of Shag Rock, it seems as if there must once have been a substantial drying rock in the present Admiralty charted position. Aerial photographs taken at low water spring tides show several rocks not far below the surface close to the charted position of Jeremy Rocks. From the outermost of these St Catherine's light bears 084° M, Shag Rock 316° M and the most left-hand of the radio aerials at Niton 033° M. They project nearly

58

The Round the Island Race fleet skirting around St Catherine's Point.

59 (above)

The rocks to the east of St Catherine's Point.

2m above the surrounding ledge and seem most likely to be what is left of the Jeremy, which, like much of the local rock, may have been quite soft. In any case a ledge of rocks, encountered more than once by Round the Island racers, reaches out westwards from the east end of Watershoot Bay, and it is significant that the local fishermen tend to keep offshore between Shag Rock and the lighthouse (Plate 58). Regrettably no satisfactory clearing transit appears to exist.

To the east of the lighthouse the shore is rocky (Plate 59) and an offlying large rock, called East St Cat's Rock, can be found 400m out when St Catherine's bears 325°M and the right-hand edge of Binnel Bay on 080° M (Plate 60).

60

East St Cat's Rock from sea level. A similar outlyer lies to the west of St Catherine's Point

St Catherine's Point is well known for its tide race, which is enhanced by the bow-shaped underwater ledge south of St Catherine's Deep. The race not only looks dramatic but is also dangerous, especially on a flood tide. For example, in 1906 the well found 24m sailing barge *Firefly* was lost there with all her crew. The worst of the race can be avoided by working along the shore, but one should be prepared for nasty overfalls off Rocken End from which there may be no escape.

Another remarkably violent tide race occurs off Bordwood Ledge (or Button Ledge) on the south side of Luccombe. It extends nearly a mile out into Sandown Bay towards the deep patch, known for some reason as Bob's Hole, and is to be particularly avoided in a southeasterly when the main Channel stream is on the ebb, otherwise an encounter with whirlpools and boiling white sea is inevitable.

As one might expect when the Channel stream is west going, a strong south-east going eddy forms under Blackgang Chine. Indeed, close into the beach the tidal stream always runs southeast, except for an hour or so after high water. Grim corroboration of this fact is provided by the old name for Reeth Bay, which used to be Wraith Bay, because so many bodies of seafarers wrecked on the west coast in the old days were carried round St Catherine's by the current, ending up in this tidal backwater. Much the same tidal effect occurs at Luccombe Bay where the tide flows south virtually all of the time.

Between St Catherine's and Steephill Cove, the tide inshore continues to flow east until an hour before high water. Between Steephill Cove and Wheeler's Bay, to the east of Ventnor, the tide inshore turns easterly after three hours of channel ebb. Thus, making to the east from St Catherine's Point against the main channel ebb tide, it will pay to hug the shore to take advantage of the slacker stream, which may turn favourable past Steephill. However, there are times when the high cliffs steal the wind, and in spite of the strong contrary tide, sailing yachts do better offshore.

From St Catherine's to Dunnose there are plenty of lobster floats to give tidal guidance but due to the strength of the flow, which tends to pull them under, they are given particularly long float lines. Thus one should be alert both to being fouled by submerged lines and to lines well up tide of their buoy. To avoid unnecessary trouble the local fishermen sometimes pull their pots close inshore for the Round the Island Race.

7 ST CATHERINE'S POINT TO DUNNOSE

Seafarers usually keep a comfortable distance clear of the coast between St Catherine's Point and Dunnose (Plate 61), and with good reason when there is a sea running onto a lee shore. Charts of the area are not so much

inaccurate, merely lacking in detail. The principal off-lying rocks are shown in the photographs but, even so, one should not push one's luck along this stretch of Island shore. Nevertheless, when the wind is very light, tidal considerations can persuade racing yachts to take risks, especially as speed over the bottom may not be enough to cause serious harm when grounding. In such circumstances a sharp bow lookout can often spot rocks, or associated weed, in time to avoid a bump; meanwhile the rest of the crew are well advised to sit down and hold on. In very settled weather one can anchor off the coves and land by dinghy. Although very rocky at low water, the principal bays have launch-ways where the rocks have been cleared. Moreover, they face due south and, arguably, receive as much sun-shine as anywhere in the country.

Once clear of St Catherine's Point, the next headland, between Reeth Bay and Puckaster Cove, is encumbered with a heavy crust of rocks not shown on the chart. The reef sticks out well to the west of the point (Plate 64) and rocks extend from the other side of Reeth Bay, giving a narrow entrance to Castle Haven, where a concrete

62

The slipway at Reeth Bay on the right.

63

Reeth Bay slipway from sea level.

ramp and small craft are to be seen (Plate 63). This is a good launching place in reasonable weather and is popular with weekend fishermen, but it does dry out to sand at low water (Plate 64). In days gone by, Reeth Bay was a fashionable spot well supplied with bathing machines, while fishing boats used the east-facing slipway at Puckaster (Plate 65); but erosion has completely taken away the protecting headland here, nor is there now much left of the old slip.

Binnel Bay lies between Puckaster and Binnel Point, and one can edge in here, keeping a wary eye on the sea ahead, the echo sounder, and the lobster pots.

64

Reeth Bay on the left and Puckaster Cove on the right, with a ledge of rocks between, looking north.

There are some formidable offshore rocks just inside the point at the west end of Binnel Bay and yet more towards the eastern end (Plates 66 and 67). If working cautiously towards the bay, large dismembered chunks of

65 (above)

Puckaster Cove, once Uffa Fox's playground.

66 (below)

The east end of Binnel Bay, looking northeast.

67 (above)
The east end of Binnel Bay from overhead.

68 (left)
The east end of Binnel Bay from sea level. The chunks of masonry on the left are remains of 'Spindler's Folly'.

masonry will be seen at the eastern end (Plate 68). These are the remains of an attempt by a German industrialist, Herr Spindler, to build a harbour in Victorian times. The walls were substantial but their foundations were on blue slipper clay so, perhaps not very surprisingly, they did not survive many gales. Little is now left of this ambitious project, known as Spindler's Folly. It should be said that he also planted hundreds of trees at Binnel

69 (above)

Rocks off the cliffs east of Binnel Point.

70 (right)

Rocks off Sugar Loaf, which can be seen on the right.

Bay and they remain as a welcome addition to the attractiveness of the area, but landing anywhere near Spindler's Folly is decidedly difficult due to numerous large submerged off-shore rocks, stretching 200m seawards of Binnel Point (Plate 69). They tend to diminish a little in number towards Woody Bay and beyond, although disconcerting outliers exist off Sugar Loaf (Plate 70), the next promontory to the west of Woody Bay (Plate 71),

with still more outliers off Woody Bay itself (Plate 72).

Woody Bay (Plate 73 and 74), though attractive, is not exactly very woody; possibly this can be explained

71 (left)

Sugar Loaf close up.

72 (below)

Binnel Point to Steephill, looking east.

73 (above)

Woody Bay on the left and Woody Point on the right.

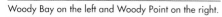

75 (above)

The prominent rock off Woody Point exposed.

76 (below)

Woody Point.

by the fact that one of its old names was Hoody Bay. There is usually access to the pebble beach from land by wooden steps, but they can be taken out by winter storms. However the slightly nimble will manage the slope very well without the steps. Landing on the large pebbles is difficult, partic- ularly at high water when the beach becomes very steep.

To the east past Woody Bay, or Dody Bay as it also once was called, will be found the inviting but inaccessible Sir Richard's Cove, which has a small pebble beach (Plate 77 and 78). The approach is rocky, particularly on

77 (right)
Sir Richard's Cove from seaward.

78 (below)
Sir Richard's Cove from the air.

the west side of the bay, so it is quite an achievement to be able to land here, even at high water. The name came from Sir Richard Worsley who lived at Appuldurcombe House. Frustrated by his inability to assist in a naval action that he had witnessed off the coast, he was consoled by King George III with a present of captured French cannon, with which he made a gun battery on the headland between the cove named after him and the adjoining Pelham Cove (Plate 79, 80 and 81). If landing at Pelham Cove at half tide, one can best come in on the line of the old slipway as it has been cleared of rocks. It

79 (above)

Pelham Cove, left, and Orchard (or St Lawrence) Cove, right.

80 (right)

Pelham Cove.

81 (left)
Pelham Cove at sea level.

82 (below)
Orchard (or St Lawrence)
Cove.

has a pleasant beach with access by a path, besides a bit of sand, though sand along this shore does tend to come and go in storms. Various breeds of animals are found above Pelham Cove, so one should not be surprised to see a llama or two.

Just to the east there is another sandy inlet, known locally as Orchard Bay (Plate 82), but named as St Lawrence Cove on old charts. On the site of the present shore-side house, there used to be a home specially built for the local excise officer in the hopes of discouraging smuggling from at least one of the Underdiff beaches. In spite of this effort, folklore suggests that the practice continued to flourish with little inconvenience. A curious smuggling sequel occurred more recently. A yacht named *Blue Hen* left Bequia in September 2002 bound for Orchard Cove, where a friend of the crew owned the house. The boat was laden with 20 bales of cocaine with a street value of £100m. The drug smugglers landed, probably by mistake, at Woody Bay about a mile short of Orchard Bay on 22 October, to walk straight into the hands of the customs, who had

83 (above)

Steephill Cove.

84 (right)

The line to approach
Steephill Cove to clear
the main ledges.

presumably been anxiously awaiting their arrival.

At Steephill Cove the entrance through the off-lying plateau of rocks faces west like an open mouth (Plate 83); it is an attractive little bay and the home of local fishing craft that operate from the beach. The none too permanent leading marks are the right hand end of a hut with three white doors

and a slender aerial on the skyline on 045°M (Plate 84). There are some rocks on this line at the outer end but, thereafter, just sand, though strong easterlies tend to sweep the sand out of the bay. The post at the entrance stands in the middle of the inner rocks, so it needs to be left well to port. There is a council slipway used for maintenance of sea defences to the east of Steephill (Plate 85) but the access road is not open to the public and anyhow launching from here is not easy.

85 (left)

The slipway to the east of Steephill. Launching from here is not easy and the access road is not open to the public.

86 (below)

Ventnor Beach, and Ventnor harbour shortly after completion. Photo ©Wightlink Gallery, courtesy of Isle of Wight County Council

87 (above)

Ventnor Harbour near high water.
Photo © Isle of Wight County Council

Ventnor is a pleasant seaside resort, and its clean sandy beach looks attractive from seaward, as indeed it is (Plate 86). If anchoring in the bay, beware the off-lying rocks at less than half tide. It should be said that these present no real problem in calm weather, provided one is careful. Once ashore, one can be certain of a warm welcome. There is a narrow man-made passage through the rocks opposite the amusement arcade and another opposite the beach steps. The derelict pier was removed in 1993.

Ventnor's small fair weather drying

88 (above)

Ventnor Harbour at low water, showing the sand bank and the fishery building, which opened in 2007. Photo © Lucy Stevens

harbour was completed in 2004 at a cost of £1.6m. It serves as an embarkation point for sailing, fishing and sightseeing craft, provides a landing point for fishermen, other than the beach, and is a tourist attraction. Two

89

Ventnor Harbour remains calm in a southwest gale, but is vulnerable from the southeast, when a storm requires that all boats in the harbour be hauled up the slipway. Photo ©Isle of Wight County Council

moorings are kept free in the centre of the harbour for visitors, which vessels of one metre draft can use two hours either side of high water. A bar of sand tends to form at the entrance of the harbour that varies in height from tide to tide (Plate 88), and the harbour is untenable when the wind is above Force 4 from the southeast.

The eight mooring buoys laid outside Ventnor's harbour are well used. They will take a vessel up to 20m (65ft) in length, though these moorings are not comfortable when the wind is above force 3. The harbourmaster has a RIB that he will use as a water taxi. He can be contacted on VHF Channel 80 and 17, or on his mobile 07976009260.

From Ventnor to Dunnose an echo sounder is of less value than usual as rocks are in random disposition and emerge steeply from a flat sandy seabed. Wheelers Bay (Plate 90) lies half a mile to the east of Ventnor at the point where the chart shows three drying rocks. In fact the bay consists

90 (above)

Wheelers Bay. Cat Rock can be seen almost on the line of the pipe on the left coming out from the shore.

91 (left)

Cat Rock.

of a large drying reef known as Ventnor Rocks with one particularly prominent one called Cat Rock (Plate 91). From Cat Rock the radio mast bears 336°M, and the edge of the headland 062° M. Further east, the stubby Church Rocks are to be found on a bed of flat sand off Bonchurch

(Plate 92). These rocks are marked on the chart and are well known, but either out of enthusiasm to evade a contrary tide, or over reliance on an echo sounder, they have brought grief to passing craft from time to time. When approaching Dunnose one can follow the curve of the coastline, but one should stay in deep water until well past the slipway at Monk's Bay, off which lie the last reef of big boul-ders. A rather beautiful full-rigged ship called the *Underley* went aground on the point between Monk's Bay and Steel Bay on 25 September 1871 in an unexpectedly strong southeasterly. Divers report that fragments of the wreck can still be seen after an onshore gale has scoured away the sand.

92

Church Rocks, Monk's Bay and Dunnose.

When Hampshire is covered in mist and murk, it often happens that the southern end of the Island is enjoying clear skies. Sandown Bay not only experiences long hours of sunshine but also is sheltered from the prevailing wind, adding to its attraction for summer visitors. Navigationally speaking, Sandown often appears to be an innocuous place, except of course in a southeasterly when it becomes like any other lee shore. Also violent gusts can come over the top of the Island in a north-westerly wind, such as capsized the sail training frigate HMS *Eurydice* on 22 March 1878 with the loss of 364 lives. After three months in the West Indies the *Eurydice* was crossing Sandown Bay in mid-afternoon under full sail with gun ports open, in what should have been the last few hours of her passage home to Portsmouth. The weather had been fine, but then an intense black cloud appeared to the north. While smaller craft in the area were taking in reefs, the crew of the *Eurydice* did not seem to have noticed. She disappeared in a violent snow squall, and when the sky cleared and the sun came out again not long afterwards only her topsails could be seen above the waves. There were two survivors.

93

Luccombe Bay from the air.

94 (above)
Luccombe Bay at sea level.

95 (left)
The public steps from the beach to the village on the clifftop.

As far as yachtsmen are concerned the old smugglers' haunt of Luccombe, within Sandown Bay, is of particular interest. It is a beautiful and often sheltered anchorage with high wooded cliffs of sandstone inter-spersed with clay. (Plate 93, 94, and 95), though one should bear in mind that the neighbouring village suffers badly from cliff erosion and landslides. To the south of Luccombe Bay, Bordwood Ledge comes out about

96 (right)
Looking south from Luccombe Bay anchorage. Bordwood Ledge lies off this point.

97 (below)
Yellow Ledge, and beyond Horse Ledge, at the north end of Luccombe Bay.

120m (Plate 96), and to the north Yellow and Horse Ledges project 200m from the shore, like a pair of devil's horns (Plate 97), their presence revealed by tidal turbulence and many lobster pot floats. A direct and central approach is best, as within the bay there is a small ledge on the south side. Even so watch out for the odd small rock in the approaches when landing on the sandy beach. Steps lead up to the top of the cliff through the chine but the steps tend to be closed after a wet winter due to landslips.

Off Shanklin Chine two buoys may be laid in the summer for visiting yachts. They are yellow, are marked 'Fisherman's Cottage' and are suitable for craft up to 12m (40ft).

Rocky patches exist close inshore at Shanklin and further north there are numerous groynes with their outer limits clearly marked with beacons. As a result of the severe storm of October 1987 – the so-called hurricane – Shanklin Pier is no more, though Sandown Pier survived (Plate 98).

The *Harry Sharman,* shown on the chart as a wreck at the east end of Sandown Bay, was an old tug which went aground in a storm in 1970 during the salvage of the burning tanker *Pacific Glory.* As the wreck is very exposed to the southwest, it has largely disintegrated, but tugs are strongly built and there is enough left of it to spoil someone's whole day (Plate 99 and 100). A rough and ready guide is to consider the tug to lie due south of Yarborough Monument, and to be a

98 (below)
Sandown Pier

99 (above)

Culver Cliff. Behind the cottages on the left is the Yarborough Monument. The offshore feature on the left is the remains of the *Harry Sharman*.

100 (left)

The wreck of the *Harry Sharman* at low water spring tide.

danger when the monument has been lost from sight behind the cliff face (Plate 101). From the stern of the wreck the bearing of the right-hand edge of Culver Cliff is 075° M, and that of the Yarborough Monument 356° M.

101
The wreck of the *Harry Sharman* is due south of the Yarborough monument and becomes a risk as soon as the monument is lost to view behind the cliff.

Whitecliff Bay is a pleasant anchorage, well sheltered from westerly winds but overshadowed by a caravan site on the cliff top (Plate 102). Approaching from the southwest, Shag Rock will be found exactly on the line of the Culver Cliffs leading out from Sandown Bay, and shows up clearly except at very high tide when it may just be covered (Plates 103 and 104).

A tiny harbour in Horseshoe Bay forms inshore of Shag Rock at high water. Thus, in very calm conditions, it is possible to go alongside the rock wall or visit the two adjoining caves looking east to Culver Spit, which are known as The Nostrils. Whitecliff Ledge dries out about 200m from the east of Culver cliff; therefore one should not cut the corner when approaching Whitecliff Bay from Sandown. Turbulent flow over the ledge gives a clear indication of the danger when the tide is running fast. It is interesting to note that a ridge of chalk forming the high downs runs right across the Island, connecting Culver Cliffs with the white cliffs of Tennyson Down. The Culver Cliff chalk is soft, and cliff falls are quite common.

102

Whitecliff Ledge off Culver Cliffs and Whitecliff Bay.

103 (above)

The end of Culver Cliffs looking northwest.

104 (below)

Horseshoe Bay and The Nostrils are at the south end of Culver Cliff. Shag Rock, which is covered, or nearly covered, at high water, is in the foreground.

Bembridge Ledge is an extensive plateau of rocks drying out 600m from the beach but sufficiently covered at high tide to cross in a small boat (Plate 105). Presence of the ledge is not at all obvious in poor visibility, and a submarine once astonished Bembridge residents by arriving there late one evening in 1968. Amongst several other visitors to the ledge was a paddle steamer called the *Empress Queen* that went aground in fog and a heavy breaking swell on 3 February 1916. In these conditions one should be especially cautious as the most prominent remains of the *Empress*

Queen are not only solid, sharp and dangerous, but lie some way out from the reef (Plate 106), as was found by two British Admiral's Cup team contenders in 1985, and even local fishing boats since.

From the wreck of the *Empress Queen* the left-hand edge of Culver Cliff bears 239° M and the coastguard lookout tower bears 333° M. It is particularly helpful to know that the wreck is on a line with the lifeboat station, just coming into view behind Bembridge on a bearing of about due

105

Bembridge Ledge, looking northeast.

106 (above)
Bembridge Ledge, looking north. The remains of the *Empress Queen* can be seen outside the ledge in the stream of beige coloured water.

107 (right)
The largest and most dangerous exposed part of the wreck of the *Empress Queen* has a spike at the top that has, in the past, been compared by sailors wrecked on it to a Stanley knife. Note that the eastern end of the lifeboat station is just coming into view from behind the point

north (Plate 107). A 1985 Admiralty Notice to Mariners gives the wreck's position as 50°40.58N, 1°04.05W, having a length of 110m, drying 1.7m and orientated on a line of 310/130°T. The Queen's Harbour Master at Portsmouth had the *Empress Queen* surveyed in 1988 with a view to disposing of the wreck with explosives, but found this to be impractical. Charts since then show the wreck more clearly just off Long Ledge.

On Admiralty charts 2022 and 2050 the coastguard tower was once

shown 200m away from its true position, which was rather confusing as it is a natural choice for taking bearings (Plate 108). However, this was amended by the Admiralty Notice to Mariners

108 (above)

A view of the Bembridge shore from the remains of the *Empress Queen*. Note the position of the box like coastguard lookout building just left of centre.

109 (below)

A view of Bembridge Ledge, looking southwest. Sharpus rocks are on the left of the picture

No 1820 of September 1987, which stated that 'the CG lookout station has moved to 50°50.88N 1°04.32W, i.e. 200m north-northeast!'.

The rocks to the east of The Run, which is the eastern sandy area that cuts through the inner ledges like a river, are called the Sharpus Rocks (Plate 109). As the name implies, they are the most rampant ones of the ledge and those most likely to cause damage. It was here that the yacht *Barracuda of Tarrant,* famous among those who followed the television series 'Howard's Way', really did go aground before dawn on 2 May 1988. She was coming home from the Royal Ocean Racing Club's Ouistreham race in a fresh southerly breeze on the port gybe, when the Princessa Shoal buoy was sighted to port quick flashing 9 every 15 seconds. This was misidentified as the Bembridge Ledge buoy, which has a characteristic of 3 flashes every 10 seconds. Experienced local seafarers say that this happens quite frequently, so it is probably easier to make this mistake than one would think.

The passage between the Princessa Shoal and the southern part of the ledge is found by lining up Culver Cliff with the high land behind Ventnor. A good safe transit is on Gatcliff, the notch in the skyline at Appuldurcombe on 249° M; but, if one has good eyesight and good visi-bility, one can take a closer course by lining up Culver Cliff with the third dip in the hills to the left of Gatcliff. At night locals use the lights of Shanklin, most of which should be in sight to the left of Culver Cliff to avoid the ledge. In daylight, when the right-hand edge of Bembridge Fort is in transit with the tower of Bembridge School on 256° M, and Nettlestone Point opens well to the right of the lifeboat house and its slipway on 326° M, one can start heading north up the channel called The Deep, between Cole Rock and the shore (Plate 110). One should be careful to avoid the mass of lobster pot floats in this area, known locally as The Minefield, and also not to become set onto the steep east side of the ledge during a spring ebb tide, which starts running two hours before high water.

Bembridge Ledge is well portrayed on the large scale charts of the eastern approaches and the harbours and anchorages. These show the bulk of the ledge to the south of the point, but in addition extensive reefs turn the corner of The Foreland, requiring the lifeboat station to be positioned well out from the shore. Less obvious are the Dicky Dawe and Cole Rocks, 600m offshore and on a transit between St Helen's Fort and Nettlestone It is a rare thing to see Cole Rock dry, but not so rare to see some craft aground there (Plate

110

Looking over Sharpus Rocks towards Bembridge
Harbour. Ethel Ledge is the ledge on which the
lifeboat station stands.

111). Dicky Dawe, by the way, was a celebrated smuggler who used to sink incoming contraband kegs on these rocks, now named after him, until he judged it safe to bring them ashore.

Over a mile out to sea, to the east of the lifeboat house, a wreck with only a 3m depth is shown on old charts. This is the remains of the destroyer *HMS Velox,* mined in 1915. The most prominent parts of the ship, such as her propeller shafts, have been salvaged and the rest of the wreck has settled into the silt, leaving little above the seabed. More modern charts show a depth of 5.3m. It is worth recording that the nearby Nab Rock, which used to have a charted depth 5.8m, now is shown with 6.8m over it. The so-called rock probably amounts to a ridge rather than a distinct feature.

Inshore, off Bembridge and Seaview there are about 32 mainly spherical yellow buoys laid in the summer as racing marks for Bembridge Sailing Club, Brading Haven Yacht Club and the Sea View Yacht Club. They stretch from opposite the Bembridge lifeboat house in the south to Nettlestone Point in the north. Whilst some of the buoys have reflective tape, only the outer eight buoys are lit, all with the characteristic Fl Y 4s. Thus by staying to the east of these lit buoys, the unlit buoys can be avoided. See Appendix I for more details.

111

Cole Rock in the foreground, virtually exposed.

Once past the line of the lifeboat pier the danger of Cole Rock is over, but there are other less prominent offshore shoal patches running parallel to Ethel and Tyne Ledges (Plate 112) in the direction of Node's Point. Half a mile to the west of the lifeboat station there is a landing place of variable convenience, depending on the state of the tide, called The Colonel's Hard. It is opposite the Bembridge Sailing Club's one-time race officer's hut, which was demolished by a tree in the October 1987 storm. In Victorian times pleasure craft used to land their passengers here and in Nelsonian times men of war, anchored in St Helen's Roads, used to land here to collect water. Old charts show The Colonel's Hard as a pier, but now it is just a slice through Tyne Ledge (Plate 113) and fragmented bits of hard. Shallow-draughted vessels can still use it for landing though it is slippery at low tide. There are three

112

Tyne Ledge in the foreground. The submerged offshore rock on the left of the picture is Garland Rock.

113

Tyne Ledge and Garland Rock on the right and St Helen's Fort on the left.

trots of private moorings off The Colonel's Hard used by the Bembridge Sailing Club for Bembridge Redwings and Bembridge One Designs. There are three visitor's buoys on the outer trot at the eastern end, designed to take yachts up to 13.6m (45ft), whose crews will be made welcome at the Bembridge Sailing Club. There is a small charge for the use these buoys. Note that the harbour water taxis cannot usually be used for landing as they do not normally go out of the harbour.

Garland Rocks emerge up to 1m from the sand southwest of St Helen's Fort and are very approximately marked by the yellow spherical racing mark with a white band, marked with a G.

BEMBRIDGE HARBOUR

With the direction of the prevailing wind as it is, Bembridge is frequently sheltered. The channel has been deepened and straightened over the years and, though there is still a bar in the entrance, making it impossible for most craft to come and go at lower states of the tide (Plate 114), there is deeper water in the harbour and the channel is well marked, though not lit. It is possible to approach St Helen's Fort (Gp Fl 3 every 10 sec, 8m) quite closely in small craft at high water but

there is a long shingle bank off the fort in the direction of Nodes Point to the east, known as 'Fort Road', and the fort has been built on an outcrop of rocks that spread a little to the east and a lot to the west. Just to the north of the fort there is a yellow post with a cross topmark and a fairly dim yellow flashing light (every 2 sec) called the approach beacon. This carries a tide gauge that gives the height of tide at the shallowest points of the channel into Bembridge Harbour, between Numbers 2 and 3A,

114

The channel into Bembridge Harbour dries out at low tide.

and just before 12 and 13 buoys. At the north end of the channel, the 0.2m diameter old sewer pipe, off the ruined St Helen's Church with its distinctive white wall, shows about 0.5m above the surrounding level. A small yellow buoy that is laid by Southern Water marks the outer end of the pipe. At the entrance of the harbour there is an old wooden breakwater on the east side, its end marked with a scaffolding post with a red wire basket on top.

115

Bembridge Harbour at low water, 17 Sep 07.
Photo ©Bembridge Sailing Club

At the Duver Marina (VHF Ch 80), built in 2004, there are 80-100 berths. Visitors can be taken of draft 1.8m (6ft) and they will remain afloat at low water springs. Craft with up to a draft of 2.4m (8ft) may be accommodated through negotiation with the harbour staff.

The berths at Fisherman's Wharf are dredged about every four years and, after dredging, will have 1.8m at low water springs, though they will silt up between dredging. The original Bembridge Marina at the far end of the harbour is reserved for permanent

mooring holders. The two deep-water moorings at the entrance of the harbour are owned by the local boatyards Attrills and AA Coombes. With permission, they can often be used on a first come first served basis. There is a high water anchorage inside the harbour on the east side. Anchoring in the channel is not allowed, and the speed limit is 6k. The two water taxis can be contacted on VHF Ch 80. The harbour and surroundings are an SSSI and are pleasant and different from other Island harbours, fully justifying a little work with the tide tables. The Harbourmaster's phone number is 01983872828.

Priory Bay, to the north of Node's Point, is an increasingly popular, pretty woodland high water anchorage (Plate 116). The bay dries out at low water so it is not wise to stay long on a falling tide, especially as it may be necessary to cross Gull Bank on the seaward side of the bay. If approaching from the north one should bear in mind the rocks off Horestone Point, which stick out about 150m.

116

The Duver Marina. Photo ©Chris Turvey

117

Seagrove Bay, Priory Bay and Bembridge Harbour, looking south.

The shallow Seagrove Bay (Plate 117) lies to the north of Horestone Point. A pleasant high water anchorage can be found clear of the rather rocky point but, at the Seaview end, rocks are more widely spread about. A particularly prominent outlying rock called Big Ben is to be found off a plateau of rocks that extends a third of a mile south from Nettlestone Point (Plate 118). Until 2001 it was marked with a red and green painted stick, but this was regularly broken and now a red cylindrical buoy, numbered 17, is laid just off Big Ben. To the north,

another red can buoy, numbered 12, marks the so-called Quay Rocks, shaped like a quay, opposite the first three houses on the point, and opposite the concrete slipway. Still further to the north, a third red can buoy, numbered 13, marks the rocks known as The Bunch, some 70m offshore. Finally a fourth red buoy, numbered 14, called Old Fort, has been established opposite the Old Fort pub and restaurant on The Esplanade, inshore of which there is a pipe above seabed

118

The ledge at the north end of Seagrove Bay. Big Ben is on the seaward side.

level that dries one metre at the shore end (Plate 119). In addition to this chain of red buoys, there are sixteen Sea View Yacht Club's racing marks off Seaview in summer, stretching from Horestone Point to No Man's Land Fort, as well as the Sea View Yacht Club's yellow starting line post so, if passing more than half a mile west of the Warner buoy at night or in poor visibility, a good lookout is necessary. See Appendix 1 for details.

Seaview makes a charming visit when the wind is from any point in the west. It is only a short dinghy trip

and a few paces to the centre of the village; but one should take care not to anchor off the Sea View Yacht Club slipway to avoid fouling telephone cables and the mooring trots of the club's Sea View Mermaid keelboats. The Sea View Yacht Club has a limited number of visitor's moorings and provides a ferry service in the summer. Take care when landing, as the large tidal range at Seaview makes for slippery steps. A wreck is shown on the chart 0.7 miles due east of Nettlestone Point, with a minimum depth of 1.1m. This was a 60m concrete barge lying north-east/south-west in a surrounding depth of 3m and, though no

119
Nettlestone Point.

Looking south southeast at The Debnigo with Seaview behind. Notice 'Radar Post' on the left of the picture.

recent encounters with it have been related, the wreck was still there when surveyed by divers in 1982. Incidentally, one of the Sea View Yacht Club's racing marks is called 'Wreck' and is marked with a 'W'. However this buoy is no longer laid anywhere near the wreck.

When planning a course from Seaview into the Solent, the short cut between No Man's Land Fort and the Island shore is an attractive option, and is always worth considering at high water. Except at high water or in shoal draft craft, one should start by steering well offshore as it quickly becomes shallow to the north of Nettlestone at a curiously shaped bank

known locally as The Debnigo, which extends from Puckpool Point towards No Man's Land Fort (Plate 120). The most obvious feature at low water is the dark coloured slim bank but in addition the bank extends south from the outer end like a flag flying. To avoid The Debnigo when leaving Seaview it may be wise to leave the yellow Sea View Yacht Club post, the Little Deb buoy and Radar Post, on the eastern tip of the Debnigo, to port. Moreover, 0.4M north of Nettlestone Point the chart shows 'obstructions'. These are lumps of metal, possibly from an early wartime barrier that

121

The Sea View Yacht Club ramp at low water spring tide. No 14 buoy is the one under the left hand ship on the horizon, and inshore of No 14 buoy, rocks and a disused and broken outfall pipe can be seen. Photo ©Andy Barrett, Sea View Yacht Club.

have impaled at least one Sea View Mermaid keelboat in the past. Nothing has been seen of these lumps of late but it may be that movement of the sand could expose them again. The tip of the Debnigo is roughly marked by a red pile at the east end of the bank, called 'Radar Post' by those who live at Ryde as, located in a previous position, it used to have radar reflectors on it. At high water, vessels of moderate draught can use Radar Post and the red Sandshead Post off the north east tip of Ryde Sands as refer-

122

Looking to the northwest from the Sea View Yacht Club. Ryde Pier can just be seen in the distance, Ryde Sands below the horizon and mark buoy sinkers in the forground.
Photo ©Andy Barrett, Sea View Yacht Club

ence points to be kept to the south but Radar Post does not mark the part of the The Debnigo that extends to the south.

Apart from numerous cables, there are also 0.3m outfall pipes exposed above sand level north of Nettlestone Point and at Spring Vale (Plate 123). The pipe north of Nettlestone Point is marked with a red buoy called Gordon. The buoy also served to mark an obstruction known as The

Bedstead. This was a wartime construction, probably the anchor for one end of an anti-submarine boom, which included metal girders of height at least one metre above the seabed, and lay roughly 150m, offshore on a line between Gillkicker and Nettlestone Point (Plate 124) but has now been removed by members of the 'Sea View Yacht Club'. The Spring Vale outfall has been shortened from 686m to 90m and is no longer marked with a buoy.

The barrier that was once shown on the chart between the Island and No Mans Land Fort no longer shows on recent charts, and the odd lumps of concrete that were found there have also been removed. Thus there is now an official channel for leisure craft on the Island side of No Man's Land Fort, intended to keep small craft out of the main fairway between No Man's Land and Horse Sand Fort. Radar Post, the post off the Debnigo (LFl R12s), and Sandshead Post (Fl R 10s), off the northeast tip of Ryde Sands, are both lit.

For information beyond this point refer to the companion volume *Solent Hazards*.

123
Looking over The Duver to The Debnigo with the Springvale outfall on the left and the Nettlestone pipe on the right.

124

The Duver Bank, northwest of Nettlestone Point. Note the position of the Sea View Yacht Club's line post – at 4 o'clock from the fort – in relation to The Debnigo.

125
The outer spit of Ryde Sands, with the Debnigo in the
background, looking southeast. The yellow SW
mining ground buoy has now been removed.

Racing Marks for Seaview and Bembridge

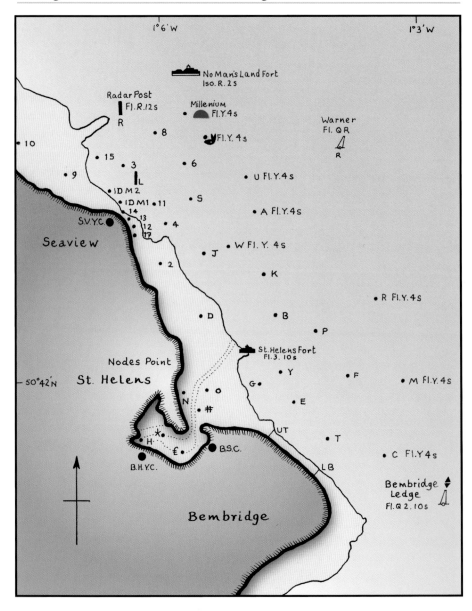

Bembridge Sailing Club and Brading Haven Yacht Club – Racing Marks

NAME	CODE	DESCRIPTION
Cochrane	C	Yellow Spherical – *Fl Y 4s*
Derrick	K	Orange Spherical
Fitzwilliam	F	Yellow Spherical
Garland	G	Yellow Spherical + White Band
Moreton	M	Orange Spherical – *Fl Y 4s*
Nainby-Luxmoore	N	Yellow Spherical
Patch	P	Yellow Spherical + Black Band
Pepe	#	Yellow Spherical
Ruthven	R	Yellow Spherical – *Fl Y 4s*
Tara	T	Yellow Spherical
Under Tyne	E	Yellow Barrel

Sea View Yacht Club Racing Marks

NAME	CODE	DESCRIPTION
Acland	A	Yellow Spherical – *Fl Y 4s*
Bertie	3	Yellow Spherical
Boom	15	Blue Spherical + white strip
Brookie	6	Blue/White Spherical
Bruce	2	Blue/White Spherical
Bunch	13	Red Can
Bunny	Bunny head	Yellow Spherical – *Fl Y 4s*
Jonah	J	Yellow Spherical
Line		Yellow Post
Little Deb	8	Orange Spherical
Lollipop	S	Red Spherical
Millennium	Blue half moon	Yellow Spherical – *Fl Y 4s*
Old 'O'	11	
Pier Head	4	Black/Orange Spherical
Quay Rocks	12	Red Can
Somers	U	Yellow Spherical – *Fl Y 4s*
Wreck	W	Yellow Spherical – *Fl Y 4s*

Seaview Outfall Marks laid by Southern Water Authority

NAME	CODE	DESCRIPTION
Big Ben	SWS (17 on chart)	Red Can
Bob	10	Red Can
Gordon	9	Red Can
Old Fort	SWS (14 on chart)	Red Can

APPENDIX 2

Hazard Points on the South Side of the Isle of Wight
(giving a seriously close point of approach, so to be used with utmost caution)

Varvassi wreck – West End	50°39.68N	001°35.57W
Irex Rock – Scratchell's Bay	50°39.55N	001°34.98W
Bench Rock – 2m line to south	50°39.54N	001°34.22W
Tank Rock	50°39.71N	001°32.99W
Adder Rock	50° 39.90N	001°31.97W
Rock south of Watcombe Bay	50°39.98N	001°30.89W
Rock east of Freshwater Bay	50°40.00N	001°30.14W
Brook Point – 2m line	50°39.01N	001°28.45W
Hardman Rock	50°38.11N	001°26.60W
Ship Ledge – 2m line	50°37.68N	001°24.30W
Off Atherfield Ledge	50°36.25N	001°21.94W
Watershoot Bay – 2m line	50°34.38N	001°18.25W
East St Cat's Rock	50°34.35N	001°17.70W
Church Rocks – west end	50°35.40N	001°11.65W
Luccombe Bay – 2m line Yellow Ledge	50°36.80N	001°09.99W
Harry Sharman wreck	50°39.72N	001°06.20W
Culver Cliff – 2m line to east	50°39.80N	001°05.30W
Empress Queen wreck	50°40.55N	001°03.98W
Bembridge Ledge – eastern tip	50°41.02N	001°03.63W
Bembridge Ledge Buoy	50°41.12N	001°02.72W
Cole Rock	50°41.43N	001°03.74W
St Helens Fort – 2m line on east side	50°42.27N	001°04.85W
No Mans Land Fort	50°44.37N	001°05.60W

INDEX

After 24 years in the Royal Navy, Peter Bruce settled in the New Forest not far from Lymington, and continues to spend much of his life on the water. In the world of yachting he is well known as a successful racing yacht owner, the revision author of *Heavy Weather Sailing*, author of local pilot books such as *Solent Tides, Solent Hazards, Wight Hazards, Tidal Streams between Portland and St Alban's Head* and *Inshore Along the Dorset Coast*, and a yacht helmsman and navigator of international calibre. He completed his first of thirteen Fastnet Races in 1961 and since then has been in the British Admiral's Cup Team as helmsman, navigator and tactician on four occasions: on two of these in the winning team, and on a third in the top individual yacht. In his own boats *Genie, The Goodies* and sundry *Owls* he has won numerous national championships, the Round the Island Race Gold Roman Bowl, and seven overall class wins at Cowes Week, besides a welter of other inshore and offshore races. He has had the distinction of winning his class in Cowes Week, Cork Week and the Scottish Series, and the rare 'double' of winning the Britannia Trophy and New York Yacht Club Trophy at Cowes Week in 1988. He remembers the fog bound Round the Island Race in the sixties, when Uffa Fox overheard the skipper and navigator of a nearby but invisible yacht discussing the likely proximity of the Island. Uffa gave an extremely realistic imitation of a dog barking that immediately caused the said yacht to tack out to sea in alarm.

Peter Bruce now does more cruising than racing, and has cruised his yachts to some of the remotest parts of the British Isles and to Ireland, Belgium, the Netherlands, Spain and France.

Peter Bruce's yacht *Owl*.

OTHER BOOKS FROM BOLDRE MARINE

SOLENT HAZARDS

The famous established work of reference for the Solent by Peter Bruce, first published in 1985, and now in its second revision of the fifth edition. The book gives pilotage data for the avoid-

ance of the Solent perils, accompanied by aerial photographs taken at extreme low water spring tide, which reveals them in a most explicit manner. The present A5-sized edition was revised in 2008 and contains a multitude of gems of Solent lore within 112 pages, in addition to about 128 colour pictures of remarkable and dramatic clarity.

ISBN 978-1-871680-31-7

INSHORE ALONG THE DORSET COAST

The highly praised mine of local knowledge by Peter Bruce, on the unusual, beautiful and interesting coast between Portland and Christchurch. The book has

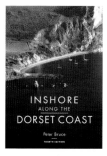

attracted a string of rave reviews and both mariners and cliff walkers have come to adore it. The A5-sized fourth edition was published in April 2008 with 136 pages and a 'feast' of 135 colour photos.

ISBN 978-1-871680-41-6

SOLENT TIDES

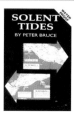

This popular tidal atlas, compiled by Peter Bruce, was a tremendous improvement upon Solent tidal stream information available up until this book was published, and has become another standard work of the Solent. It gives excellent detail, both in the main fairways and where eddies form along the shore. It is printed on durable plastic waterproof paper that is not only impermeable but is also almost impossible to tear. The third much revised A5-sized edition was published in 2008.

ISBN 978-1-871680-56-0

TIDAL STREAMS BETWEEN PORTLAND BILL AND ST. ALBAN'S HEAD

Modern technology has brought some new and very accurate tidal stream data to this popular coastline, thanks to HR Wallingford and Amoco, British Gas, BP and Elf. This tidal atlas by Peter Bruce and Gillie Watson is a big improvement on previous information available, particularly close inshore. Printed upon 18 pages of impermeable and tear resistant polyethylene A5-sized waterproof paper and published in January 1998.

ISBN 978-1-871680-16-4

All obtainable from:
BOLDRE MARINE
Kestrel Cottage • Shirley Holms
Lymington • Hampshire • SO41 8NH • UK
Telephone and Fax +44(0)1590683106

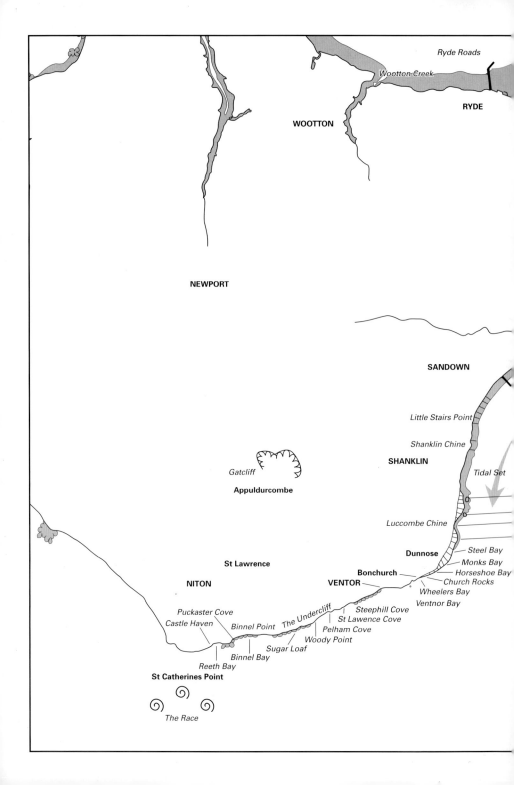